D1177142

YOU GOTTA ASK

How to Have Meaningful Conversations
With Anyone Using Compelling Questions

Jon and Pam Strain

You Gotta Ask
*How to Have Meaningful Conversation With Anyone Using
Compelling Questions*
By You Gotta Ask, Inc. © 2021

Cover Concept and Logo Design: Tyler Penner Design
Cover and Interior Design: Fusion Creative Works, FusionCW.com
Lead Editors: Megan Terry and Heather Goetter
Book Production: Aloha Publishing

Softcover ISBN: 978-1-7365901-0-2

Published By: You Gotta Ask, Inc.

Printed in the United States of America

C*NTENTS

To everyone who wants to be compelling and forthright sharing the amazing grace of Jesus.

INTR*●*DUCTION

Compelling questions get your attention and keep you thinking.

You Gotta Ask is about using compelling questions to create meaningful conversations that begin transformation in people's lives by steering them toward Christ. This book is a roadmap, and the end goal is to populate God's kingdom with people and make friends for the eternal future.

Most people have significant God and life questions they rarely explore well, so they welcome a relational setting to unpack their questions and discover meaning in their lives and struggles. People tend to live their lives in patterns and don't stop to think about many subjects that fall outside those patterns. A compelling question hijacks the brain by breaking that pattern and causing them to think about the question and explore a topic more deeply than they would have otherwise.

The greatest problem people face today, and have ever faced, is the problem of fear. Fear is our tangible response to the enemy, to death, and to separation from God. It's often used as a tool against us and can keep us from developing better relationships with each other and with God.

You Gotta Ask represents a solution within its name:

You: We are Christ's witnesses, but we're often paralyzed by fear, which keeps us from sharing the gospel. We don't know how to invite people into meaningful conversations about God and life.

Gotta: As Christians, we're called to share the gospel. It's a command, and it's imperative because lives are perishing and people need our help.

Ask: Questions provide a prompt for us to examine our own faith and steer others to Christ.

You Gotta Ask provides a tool for people to reach others through empathy and curiosity. It starts with simple, sticky questions you can pop into conversations with an easy lead-in. The questions can lead very quickly to fascinating and meaningful discussions.

The trajectory of my life changed because someone asked me a compelling question. My story illustrates why I employ compelling questions to share the grace of Jesus. I knew I was perishing, and a compelling question disrupted my life and got me to think about my faith.

On a spring day after school, I was driving and talking with my girlfriend, Karen, when we turned into a cemetery. It was my senior year of high school, and my focus was fulfilling the Schlitz Beer company motto—"You only go around once in life, so go for all the gusto!"—in an attempt to medicate my despairing soul. I was frustrated and experiencing a lot of pain over broken family and general despair about the point of life. We found ourselves having a bizarre conversation about death. Karen was not religious, but she was testing some eclectic ideas about death. She asked, "What do you think will happen to you when you die?"

My response surprised us both. I said tersely, "I don't know and I'm tired of this conversation. Let's get the hell out of here!"

Her curiosity crushed, we departed the cemetery and that was the end of the conversation—for us, but not for me. I couldn't help but wonder why I'd had such a disproportionate and blistering response to her sincere curiosity.

As a "confirmed Lutheran," it was a question I should have been able to answer, but I could not face the dreadful sense that I was perishing. My heart toward God was hard. Some people have intellectual or emotional barriers to faith; mine was volitional, simply wanting to run my own life. Yet I felt profoundly lost.

Karen's compelling question latched onto my soul for the next two months. When I moved to Palm Desert, California, for a job, I began to realize that my war was with myself. I found the answer to her compelling question when I tapped into the deep resources of God through Jesus. I'll tell that story later in the book. Since then, I've become a guide for others.

Karen had no idea her question would permanently alter my life's trajectory. But questions hijack the brain—they get your attention and keep you thinking. Compelling questions are like gold, but one specific question is like platinum, a precious metal rarer than gold. This unique Platinum Question is adaptable, effective, and always evokes a thoughtful response.

The Platinum Question is not the only compelling question you can use to initiate spiritual conversations, but it is my go-to question. This question has led to spiritual conversations with thousands of people for many years. It's a fun and fascinating first step on a conversational road map, followed by a sequence of six more explorational questions you can use to guide others to eternal life. We don't say enough about the importance of prayer, the Holy Spirit, and mastering the gospel in this book. But we feel most of these things have already been said in other evangelism books. The point of this book is to get you activated and sharing the gospel. It's much easier than you think to get people talking and thinking about God.

"Here's the lesson: Use your worldly resources to benefit others and make friends. Then, when your possessions are gone, they will welcome you to an eternal home." —Jesus, Luke 16:9 (NLT)

H💬W TO READ THIS BOOK

This book is designed in a very unique way. It allows the reader to follow along with both the teaching and the corresponding story on the same page. Use it like a reference: read all or part of the teaching, then switch to the story that illustrates the teaching, and then switch back again.

In each chapter, the upper portion of each page contains the questions and learning section. This is the area that will explain the compelling question and challenge you to try asking questions yourself. The learning section moves from the top half of one page to the top half of the next page.

The bottom portion of each page shares a true story about how God used compelling questions to bring a searcher one step closer to Him. These sections are set up in the same format as the learning sections—they move from the bottom half of one page to the bottom half of the next page. Each chapter ends in Sound Bites, which summarize the chapter.

We hope you enjoy this unique style. Let us know how you put to action what you learn and experience.

PART ONE

Compelling questions are open-ended, unbiased, and reveal what we long for.

Compelling (adj): evoking interest, attention, or admiration in a powerfully irresistible way.

Compelling questions grab your interest and stick with you. They're irresistible. People want to answer them. So what is the Platinum Question?

· ·

Assuming there is a God, and you could ask God anything, what would you ask?

· ·

How would you answer this question yourself? Take a moment to think and write down your first thought—just a simple question or even a single-word subject. There is no right or wrong answer.

....

....

....

What question do you think most people would ask?

....

....

....

What would your spouse, best friend, children, or roommate ask?

....

....

....

The reason this question is so effective is that it's non-threatening and compelling. People want to answer it. It's phrased in an open-ended and judgment-free

STORY: HEY GUYS, WATCH THIS!

Usually the phrase "Hey guys, watch this!" precedes a dude doing something stupid. Another version is, "Hold my beer." These phrases get our attention because we want to witness the spectacle.

I was with eight men at a coffee house, concluding an early morning discussion, when the server walked toward us with the check. I said, "Hey guys, watch this!" They quieted down.

way, allowing them to respond genuinely. It's a valuable tool for witnesses of Christ because it's simple and memorable, and the set-up and follow-up are easy. Simply ask and listen, and you can circle back later when the person has had some time to think about it.

It also gives us the opportunity to learn about the person we're asking so that we can spark an interesting discussion. This question exposes how a person is experiencing God and their barriers to faith. In the following chapters, we'll cover five follow-up questions. But even if you don't have the opportunity to ask the follow-up questions, this question alone will stick in someone's mind and get them thinking.

STORY

"Sam," I said to the server, "You've overheard us talking about God and life questions. I'd like to hear your brief reaction to an interesting question. I'm not looking for a correct answer, but just your answer."

"Okay," she replied.

"Assume there is a God for this question. And you have the opportunity to ask any question you want or

 CONTINUED . . .

DO · THIS · NOW

Put this book down and text someone the question. Practice asking. Cast your line into the water.

"Fortune favors the bold." —Virgil, the poet

Here is a script you can speak into the text box if you're not sure what to say:

"Hey! I'm reading a book and found this compelling question. How would you answer it? I'll share mine after you share yours. Deal? 'Assuming there is a God, and you could ask God anything, what would you ask?'"

STORY

take God to task on any issue. What would your question or subject be? No need to get into it, just give us the question or subject."

"Whoa!" Her eyes darted to where the ceiling and wall met in front of her. She paused. "Why?"

The men were taken aback by the intensity of her question, which seemed to have come from the depth of her soul.

When you get a response, would you share the questions you get by text or email with me? I'm keeping a tally to write a guide exploring the most asked questions. Text me at (208) 440-6645 or email jstrain@ YouGottaAsk.com.

☐ *Practice by texting someone the question*

☐ *Email or text Jon about the response you received*

☑ *That was easy*

STORY

"Why what?"

"Why am I here? What is the point of it all?" she asked.

All eight men watched with astonished saucer-sized eyes as she elaborated. As Sam concluded, I said, "Thank you. Yours is a very important question." My intention was simply to listen and affirm her for taking the risk to answer.

 CONTINUED . . .

"The important thing is to not stop questioning. Curiosity has its own reason for existing."

—*Albert Einstein*

STORY

As soon as she departed, the men reacted.

"Did you set that up?"

"I can't believe you just did that and she just said that!"

"Why did you do this?"

"That was so simple! I could do that!"

SOUND BITES

● Compelling questions are open-ended, unbiased, and reveal what we long for.

● The Platinum Question exposes how a person is experiencing God and their barriers to faith. A.W. Tozer says, "What comes into our minds when we think about God is the most important thing about us."

● When you ask a question, listen well. Listening reveals what to do next. You may be amazed at how obvious the next step might be.

STORY

I explained to them, "For several years I've used this question with seekers and skeptics. It's compelling and always evokes a response."

Most people are privately wondering about significant God questions. The opportunity to voice them and be listened to without judgment is very rare. Learning how people are experiencing God informs us how to invite them to take the next step.

Compelling questions invite us to share our stories and empathize with each other.

The Platinum Question sparks a conversation and ignites our curiosity. The conversation can go anywhere from there, but there are a number of compelling follow-up questions that are helpful to continue the discussion while steering us toward Christ.

I like to follow up with this question next:

. . . .

So, of all the questions you could have asked,
why ask this one?

. . . .

What's behind your answer to the Platinum Question?

....

....

....

Asking this question gives us context into what the other person is experiencing in their life. It helps us understand and empathize. Do you feel frustrated when people judge you for things without understanding the broader context of your life? Nothing alienates more than being misunderstood. People want to be explored with empathy.

Context is vital to interpreting any narrative or text. Without context, we misread each other and respond inappropriately. Our responses may be harsh, dismissing, or judgmental. James 1:19 says, ". . . *everyone must be quick to hear, slow to speak . . .*" This verse tells us to listen well and 'zoom-out' to see the bigger picture.

STORY: ADVENTURE DINNER

Pam and I like to create relational settings to ask and explore compelling questions, such as the Adventure Dinner, a four-course meal with a discussion theme for each course. The connection over fine food and fascinating conversation over the first two courses readies the guests for the third course, when we ask the Platinum Question.

Listening well allows us to identify barriers to faith: emotional, intellectual, and volitional. Knowing a person's barriers will give us direction when we invite them to take a next step toward God.

When I attended the funeral of a friend's wife, who had suffered from mental illness, I was surprised by how beautifully my friend spoke of her. "To speak of my wife and her life, we need to think of it as 'the book of Leslie.' If we only focused on the dark final chapters, we would not have a clear picture of the woman I fell in love with, her giftedness, and contributions."

Our lives are full and complex, and no one person can truly know everything about us. We reveal some parts of our lives to each other, but certain parts are

STORY

Most guests want to dive into explaining their answer immediately, but I request restraint until each one gives their question or topic. And as the host, I find that it is better if someone specifically asks what my question is rather than me volunteering it, because my question is a good segue to discussing something inviting about God. *"God, why aren't you more obvious in revealing yourself to us? Why so obscure?"*

 CONTINUED . . .

in lockdown, where much of our pain, shame, and guilt reside.

Will you be a safe listener, treating people's stories as sacred ground and respecting their boundaries? When you're empathetic and listen well, you can become a relational influencer to that person. They'll become more open to discuss ideas with you and explore their own ideas, beliefs, and faith.

STORY

One night no one asked what my question to God would be. I restrained myself from bringing it up and focused on listening and trusting God for outcomes. One woman had been prickly and snarky throughout the dinner. She shared a troubling experience with a clergyman. Instead of challenging her interpretation of the experience (which she could have felt was judgmental) I took an approach of empathy by saying,

DO · THIS · NOW

Circle back with the person you texted and ask, "So, of all the questions you could have asked, why ask this one?" Listen and enjoy their story.

☐ *Connect with your text recipient*

STORY

"I'm sorry this happened to you, but I'm really glad you shared it and got it off your chest."

After dinner, the woman expressed relief about the evening. "I was nervous all week. I kept thinking about what was going to be talked about and if I could keep from swearing. Now after this dinner I am hoping to have another similar dinner where I'll bring up these questions and ask what the Bible says about these

CONTINUED . . .

SOUND BITES

- Compelling questions invite us to share our stories and empathize with each other.

- Everyone wants to be understood with sincerity and within the context of their life.

- Listen with curiosity while respecting their sacred ground.

- Limit talking to asking questions, clarifying, and exploring with curiosity.

- Ask permission to ask.

STORY

issues." Pam and I were stunned at her dramatic flip in tone and openness.

Compelling questions invite us to share our stories and empathize with each other.

Request our complimentary *Adventure Dinner* handbook in PDF by emailing jstrain@YouGottaAsk.com.

*Compelling questions create curiosity,
which allows us to be open to new ideas.*

The questions that we would like to ask God are often things beyond our control or outside our understanding. They expose our frustrations, insecurities, and beliefs. Once we've thought of the question, it's hard to stop thinking about it. It begs to be answered. To encourage deep thinking about the question, it's helpful to ask this:

· ·

How would you answer this question for
yourself right now?

· ·

How you would answer *your own question* for God?

....

....

....

....

Many people answer, "I have no idea."

Sometimes they volley the question back, wanting to hear my answer. We gain a sense of catharsis when we feel heard, which makes us more open to others' ideas. Compelling questions beg us to share with others as we think them through.

But there's a problem. In our distracted culture, people struggle to think and reflect. A former professor of mine jestingly said, "5% of people think. 15% think they think. 80% would rather die than think." Many distractions keep us from thinking through questions of faith.

A second problem is that, as Christians, we often distance ourselves from seekers and skeptics for fear of being exposed as not having the answers. "What if

STORY: FRIENDSHIPS FOR ETERNITY

After my conversion to Christ, I attended Idaho State University. Looking for people who shared my relationship with Jesus, I stepped into a gold mine of willing mentors such as a student named Rich, who invited me to play pickup football. There, I met Mark, a campus ministry staff member, who invited me to church, where Pastor Mike adeptly taught a Bible text in an enlightening way. When Mark introduced me to

they ask me something I don't know?" Thankfully, while Jesus said, "You shall be My witnesses." (Acts 1:8) He did not specify that we must be *expert* witnesses.

As a new Christ-follower in college, I was certainly no expert, but I adopted a habit of letting other people's questions be a stimulus for my own investigation and growth. It's freeing to say, "I don't know, but what a great question. I need to answer it for myself." I later circled back with those individuals to share my research.

Another paralyzing problem that keeps us from sharing our faith and asking faith questions is dogmatism. We're afraid of being perceived as opinionated and intolerant. Our culture doesn't like people who come across as having answers or possessing certitude. People are desperately looking for answers,

STORY

Pastor Mike, he included a brief sketch of my spiritual journey.

Mike's piercing brown eyes matched his penetrating question, "Jon, suppose you died and found yourself standing before God, who asked, 'Jon, why should I let you into heaven?' What would you say?"

CONTINUED . . .

but we're cautious to offer answers because we're afraid we'll be dismissed for such arrogant certitude. We find it more endearing when others are authentic about their limitations, yet we also don't trust them if they appear incompetent on a subject matter.

If we follow 1 Peter 3:15, "Always being ready to make a [reasoned] defense to everyone who asks you to give an account for the hope that is in you," what do we do? Exhibit humility through openness and curiosity while remaining committed to being competent in the subject matter. It's fun and fascinating to engage people in compelling questions that explore faith. You'll have the opportunity to share a couple points of evidence, and then invite a reply with, "Now, I'd like to hear what you think."

STORY

It was intimidating to be put on the spot by an apparent biblical scholar. Tepid and uncertain, I replied, "Because He died for me?"

Generously, Mike said, "Jon, that's as good of an answer as one could give." This question stimulated in me an openness to grow. Mark and Rich became great friends and wise guides over the next two years as I continued to explore the question deeper.

. . . END

Our road map consists of compelling questions that create curiosity, which allows openness to new ideas. These types of questions are inviting to people with a post-modern mindset, who see themselves as self-authorities on all things.

DO · THIS · NOW

☐ *Text, email, or ask in person the third question.*

"I'm curious, how would you go about answering your question for yourself right now?"

In a sentence, how did they answer you? (Silence? No worries. They're thinking.)

....

SOUND BITES

- Use questions to spark curiosity, which stimulates openness to learn and discover new ideas.

- Practice humility by hearing other people's questions and seeking answers to those questions for yourself.

- Research the question and share with the questioner a few brief points on what you gleaned. Listen to their reaction.

- Be humble and move toward competence rather than arrogant certainty.

*Compelling questions allow us to listen
well and guide others.*

The fourth compelling question encourages us to find a guide and continue to seek answers beyond what we're able to answer for ourselves.

. . . .

Do you know anyone who could guide you,
or a resource you can consult, to find an
answer to your question?

. . . .

Who comes to mind? In what part of life do they guide you? How does the transfer of wisdom happen?

....

....

....

It's important to seek out mentors to answer life questions. Isolation or untrustworthy mentors can cause us to draw the wrong conclusions. Reaching out to others helps you answer your questions and challenge your beliefs and biases. It gives you a sounding board and another perspective to consider.

Who can we trust, respect, and learn from? Most of us learn much on the internet but lack context to discern if the source is a wise person, a foolish person, or an evil person trying to take advantage of us. My mentors have faces and I know about their lives. I want to see and hear how their ideas work out in their lives and hear about their failures and the process they went through to gain wisdom.

We're also becoming increasingly isolated from community and relationships. We like our private space, creaturely comforts, and devices. Canadian philosopher Charles Taylor describes our lives as focused

STORY: FINDING MENTORS

Mark, the campus ministry guy, took the opportunity to create a foundation of knowledge for my limited understanding of the Bible. He introduced me to the *Transferable Concepts*. Opening the booklet's cover, Mark read two passages.

"Go, therefore, and make disciples of all the nations, baptizing them in the name of the Father and the Son

within an "immanent frame." Immanent refers to the here and now—essentially, we're limited to our immediate perception of the world. I spend a good deal of my day checking my phone: texts, emails, weather, time, news, information about everything. All of it is focused on the here and now. I control it, but through the signals and prompts, I am controlled by addictive triggers to constantly check it.

So many of us live in a state of mind and lifestyle where we're bunkered down with our devices, isolating ourselves from problems and people. We're also isolating ourselves from life, relationships, and exploring transformational ideas.

Pam hosted a discussion with younger women to explore significant God and life questions. The women

STORY

and the Holy Spirit, teaching them to follow all that I commanded you . . ." —Matthew 28:19-20

"The things which you have heard from me in the presence of many witnesses, entrust these to faithful people who will be able to teach others also." —2 Timothy 2:2

CONTINUED . . .

had mixed worldviews but loved having a glass of wine and talking freely about their questions without judgment. When Claire was invited, she felt liberated from her bunker of feeling lonely. She said, "That night changed the trajectory of my journey. It was absolutely the best night, one that lifts you up, encourages your spirits, challenges your norms, and lights a fire under you. It was a let's-do-this-life-thing-and-let's-do-it-together kind of feeling. I was reminded of my worth, what my identity really means, and it brought to life the concept of community."

Just like Claire, we all need community and the mentorship of others to feel connected and to explore compelling questions outside the bunkers of our own minds.

STORY

We would review the *Transferable Concepts* in a weekly Bible study together, because part of mastering a concept is sharing with others. Week by week, I awkwardly engaged the reading. Anything new and worth doing is awkward at first: playing an instrument, algebra story problems, golf, or studying the Bible. Friendship and practice minimize awkwardness.

40

DO · THIS · NOW

Who can you invite to lunch or coffee by simply saying, "I've never really heard your story." Listen curiously and make sure you don't hijack the conversation by turning it to you.

☐ *Invite a friend to share their story*

STORY

Mark was fun, loved sports, and created relational space to ask questions. He introduced me to Paul Little's *Know Why You Believe* and Josh McDowell's *More Than a Carpenter* and *Evidence That Demands a Verdict.* I discovered many significant Christian scholars and thinkers like C.S. Lewis whose ideas loaded my college papers and my life.

 CONTINUED . . .

SOUND BITES

- Compelling questions bring people out of their bunkers of isolation and get them to engage with others in meaningful discussion and stretch their ideas beyond what they could discover on their own.

- Compelling questions allow us to listen well and guide others.

- We all need community and the mentorship of others to feel connected and to explore questions outside the bunkers of our own minds.

STORY

But even the best and wisest mentors, professors, parents, and guides have limitations. To whom shall we go for our ultimate questions and challenges? We'll explore the answer to that in the next compelling question.

Compelling questions give us the opportunity to take risks we wouldn't otherwise take.

The fifth compelling question challenges us to take a risk and test our beliefs. It encourages us to do more than just think about our answers by reaching out to God.

. . . .

Have you ever thought to simply and directly ask God your question?

What have you got to lose?

. . . .

Think for a moment. What possible reasons would cause you *not* to ask? Do your hesitations have to do with something you believe about God's deficiencies? Or do your hesitations have more to do with you?

....

....

....

Asking God a question is one of the simplest and hardest things to do. It takes only a matter of seconds, but we're often intimidated by what the response might be. If God answers, then we can no longer deny that He is there.

God doesn't violate our freedom. He allows us to make our own decisions and live our lives the way we want. We have to make the choice to reach out and ask, and many people make the choice to ignore God. With the amount of free will we have, God's plan can seem confusing and chaotic to us, making it hard to relate to someone we know so little about.

One morning at Starbucks, a man named Eldon asked a difficult question. Several Idaho guys would routinely gather at the same table and talk about

STORY: A SIGN FROM GOD

A mutual friend introduced me to Randy, an atheist, after he showed interest in our upcoming skeptic's forum. Randy joined about fifty people packed into a large home for this event. The promo line for the forum was, "If you're a believer, bring a skeptic. If you're a skeptic, bring a believer." At the end of the evening, Randy asked the final question to our guest scholar, "What difference has God made in your life?"

everything. They were not shy about disagreeing. I knew a couple of them, so they invited me to join them. Eldon served as a Captain in Vietnam. After a few months of sizing me up at these meetings, he picked a fight.

"I have a question for you!" he said loudly, pointing his finger at me. The other six guys went quiet as he spent nearly three minutes verbally packing everything wrong on planet earth into a messy ball of tangled wires. Finally, someone else asked, "Eldon, is there a question in this somewhere?"

I said, "Eldon, there are at least nine issues in this question. I don't even know where to begin!"

He said, "Start anywhere!"

STORY

At our first meeting after the forum, I said, "Randy, tell me your story." Randy had a hunger for real answers, so for several weeks we met one-on-one to work through his questions. He revealed to me months later that before we met, he'd taken a necessary risk and reached out to God. One night, he prayed, "God, if you are there, show me a sign."

     CONTINUED . . .

So I plunged in. The issues he brought up turned into multiple discussions over the next few months. One day, I asked Eldon the Platinum Question. He roared, "I would tell God there is something wrong with His business plan!"

I suggested he bring his frustration and anger to God. God can handle our rage.

After the men left one morning, Eldon revealed the source of his question. He was trying to reconcile his emotions with Vietnam and the lives lost by his bullets in service to his country. I listened empathetically. I had no satisfying answer. There was only God's amazing grace to offer.

As humans, we can't discover all the answers to our questions, and we can't fully understand God's plan.

STORY

The sign came faster than he expected. The next morning he received a sign—literally! Driving to work he saw a billboard reading, "You asked for a sign. Here's your sign. —God." I asked him what he thought when he saw it. His answer was a four-letter expletive.

"What did you do with this?" I asked.

"Nothing. I didn't know what to do with it."

Ultimately, to get the answers and the peace we seek, we must turn to God. The fifth compelling question asks us to take a risk and speak to God, not knowing what kind of response we will get.

DO · THIS · NOW

Ask God your question. What do you have to lose? Maybe you have asked but haven't heard from God. Ask yourself, "Have I responded to the last thing God said to me?" He answers prayers, and not just the prayer itself, but how we relate to Him throughout our lives.

☐ *Ask God your question*

STORY

"You drove this route to work five days a week. What are the odds the sign had just been put up or you'd never noticed it before?"

"I know," he said resignedly. Over a year later, after months of conversation, Randy asked for a second sign. He received an answer on his next walk. It was a glowing cross on a neighbor's house.

CONTINUED . . .

SOUND BITES

- Asking God your life and faith questions directly is one of the best ways to find answers. God tends to answer our prayers through circumstances and people in our lives.

- We cannot ask of others what we have not ourselves done. Ask God your own question first, and then invite others to do the same.

- Use compelling questions to invite others to take risks. "What have you got to lose?"

STORY

Have you ever simply and directly asked God your question? Have you invited others to do the same? People may hesitate to ask God directly because they're afraid of what might happen, but sometimes they may not even believe they can or are allowed to question God. But asking God directly is one of the best ways to get answers. He may not always answer, at least in the way we expect, so it's important to pay attention and be open to answers.

. . . END

*Compelling questions replace "I don't know,"
with "I will ask."*

The sixth compelling question makes us think about who God is. It gives us the chance to reconcile what we desire and our innate sense of God with God's true character.

. . . .

For you to be a praying person,
what would you need God to be like?

What attributes do you need God to possess?

What moral perfections and superpowers
would make God "God" for you?

. . . .

This may sound blasphemous, but let's create a God.

What attributes *should* God have to be worthy of your trust?

Moral characteristics God must have:

....

....

....

Superpowers God must have:

....

....

....

When we've led groups through the "create a God" exercise, they discover the God of the Bible intuitively. The attributes they write down describe the character of the biblical God. As with all the compelling

STORY: CALLED BY GOD

Randy was prompted to ask God for a sign by the "create a God" exercise. But prior to that, Randy and I met for coffee again. This time, he was less guarded and more open, and he told me about a book he was reading. "I think I agree with the author's notion that all of us have a calling," he said.

I wondered if he was aware of the implications of this idea. I took out my yellow pad and suggested we unpack

questions we've outlined, this exercise exposes our wants and needs. Nobody wants a solution until they understand they have a problem.

Through the "create a God" exercise, we uncover our needs and desires. The questions leading up to this exercise help us examine our problems before we address a solution, which allows us to be more open to hearing it. The exercise illustrates how perfectly God fits as the solution to our wants and needs.

While many people may hesitate to reach out to God and question him directly, we can see through God's attributes that He is worth praying to. When we know to whom we're praying, it becomes easier to ask directly. Rather than saying "I don't know," we are given

STORY

the idea. I said, "Randy if a person is 'called,' does that not imply there is someone doing the calling?"

"I guess it does," he said.

I wrote down "caller."

"Would this someone be personal and have intelligence?"

the freedom to say, "I will ask." We are empowered to seek answers to our questions.

In the previous story, when Randy risked asking God for a sign a second time, he received a customized answer through the glowing cross on his walk. It was like God was asking, "Randy, I'm here, but where are you?" This time, Randy responded.

The sign let Randy know he was not alone. He'd experienced another sign before but had ignored it until then. God doesn't crowd us. He seeks to draw us in. God wants us to respond authentically and bring him our objections, so that He can help us solve our problems and answer our questions.

STORY

"It seems reasonable."

I wrote that down too.

"Wouldn't it also imply this someone is a designer and creator with a purpose?"

"I guess so," he replied, warily watching words populate on the page in my hands.

DO · THIS · NOW

Using the questions in this chapter, have fun practicing the "create a God" exercise in a small group or at the dinner table.

☐ *Practice the "create a God" exercise*

STORY

"Wouldn't it also imply He has good and benevolent intentions toward those He calls?" At this point, Randy stopped answering, but I continued, "Wouldn't it also imply that He is powerful enough to make the calling happen? And can we assume He would be fair and just in His distribution of callings?"

By this point, a list filled over half of the yellow page full of descriptors that would be required to support his in-

        CONTINUED . . .

*"The Lord is gracious and compassionate;
slow to anger and great in mercy."*

—King David (Psalm 145:8)

STORY

tuition that people have a calling. The problem was apparent: Randy was painfully separated from the Caller.

"Randy, all these descriptive words are attributes of the God of the Bible. The Bible also says He loves you and has a purpose, plan, and calling for your life. Next time we get together, I'd like to describe for you as clearly as possible how He has made this possible. Could we meet again for this purpose?"

SOUND BITES

- The "create a God" exercise helps replace "I don't know" with "I will ask."

- People are God-coded—we intuitively know His attributes.

- Watch for signs from God. When you don't know the answer to a question, ask.

STORY

By examining Randy's idea that people have a calling, we were able to ask questions he otherwise wouldn't have asked. Compelling questions replace "I don't know" with "I will ask." Unsure what he believed, Randy eventually asked God for a second sign and received it: a glowing cross one of his neighbors had just put up when he was on his evening walk.

PART TWO

Compelling questions need a relatable lead-in.

How do we create a lead-in to bring up the Platinum Question and other compelling questions? Start by establishing rapport through small talk.

Small talk is important because it allows you to test the temperature of the conversation with respect. During small talk, we're subconsciously asking, "Do you like me? Do I like you?" In every conversation, we are always reading the level of warmth and openness below the surface, and neutral topics like the weather or sports give us a safe space to do this.

When I begin a conversation, I find out a person's name first. People love to hear their name and asking gives you a head start. Then I like to give some brief context to reveal why I'm curious about them and why I'm thinking about the compelling question.

Lead-ins serve to overcome awkwardness. Here are three lead-ins you can use or adapt to your personal style:

1. Generic Lead-In

"I have something I'd like to ask you. I was [listening to speaker, reading a book, meeting with a group of friends] the other day and a very interesting question was raised. I'd like to hear how you would answer it."

There is usually some level of acknowledgement.

"I don't know what you believe, but the question assumes there's a God. Say you can ask God any question you want, and get a response, or you can take God to task on a subject. You don't have to get into it, but what would your question or subject matter be?"

STORY: GOD IS RESPONSIBLE FOR THE RESULTS

At a diner, my friend Richard and I learned our table server's name and asked for her counsel on the best menu items. Inviting someone to share their expertise and special knowledge is great for building rapport.

When she brought the check and began to remove our plates, I said, "Richard and I meet with some guys to explore God and life questions. I'd like to hear your reaction to perhaps the most interesting ques-

2. Brief Lead-In

My friend Jenni Byrd offered this lead-in: "The other day, someone asked me an awesome question."

A pause will usually draw a reciprocating, "What was it?"

"Assuming there is a God and you can ask God any question . . ."

3. Bold Lead-In

My friend Jim is bolder than I, and it's been very fruitful for him. He actually uses the name "Jesus Christ" when he asks the Platinum Question,

STORY

tion we've explored. This is not a 'correct answer' kind of question. It simply invites your special answer. Assuming there's a God..."

Holding our heavy plates, she said, "I've got to think about it for a moment. Let me take these plates to the kitchen and I'll return with an answer."

She returned with another employee and said, "I asked her the question and she wants to answer it, too."

     CONTINUED . . .

which is higher risk than more generically saying "God."

He'll say, "Let's say Jesus Christ is standing right here and you can ask him any question you want and get an answer. What would you ask him?"

People are often hungrier and more open than we realize.

STORY

Mostly, we listened and affirmed the value of each question. This was the right thing to do in this setting. Perhaps there will be an opportunity to circle back, but it's okay to simply let the question work and trust God to use it in His own time and way. God is responsible for the results.

DO · THIS · NOW

Choose or prepare your own lead-in.

....

....

....

....

....

....

....

....

....

....

SOUND BITES

- Be curious about others. When in doubt, ask permission to ask.

- Use a person's first name in conversation.

- Give context to clarify your motive in your lead-in.

Written by Pam Strain

As you can probably tell by now, there are a number of ways to ask compelling questions about God and life. Jon has a fairly direct style, but my style differs from his. If you're not comfortable asking questions as directly as Jon does, you might find my approach easier to manage.

The question I most often use is not truly a question. It is this:

Tell me your story.

People are usually eager to share when you ask. This approach comes naturally to me because I'm curious about people. When people tell their stories, it gives me the opportunity to listen and look for common ground.

I've shared my own story so many times it's easy to find common ground when listening to others. My story largely revolves around how I was like a chameleon—I would just adapt to whatever circumstances I was in at the time. The bottom line was that I was looking to be loved, and that's something that comes up frequently—I hear it in almost every person's story.

Everybody has a story, and the challenge is getting them to talk about it. Often they don't talk right away, so you have to try a few different types of questions until something reaches that person.

Everyone has barriers to what they're willing to share. For someone who has an intellectual barrier rather than an emotional one, they may resonate more with the direct questions. But you don't necessarily know that when you're talking to someone, so it requires discernment and practice to know what to ask. Test these approaches out and see what you're most comfortable with and what others find comfortable. It

STORY: WHO ARE YOU ASKING?

Someone invited Andrina to one of my discussion groups. She's in her forties, single, and has an 11-year-old child. The two of us went for coffee, and I had already discerned that she was open and curious about the topics we were discussing. I asked her if faith played a role in her life.

She told me that she was raised in a very legalistic Christian home. When she got a divorce, her parents

may take some experimentation to figure out a style of questioning that works well for you.

One of my favorite variations is to ask, "Tell me a little bit about what makes you you. What's been formative in your life to get you where you are today?"

After they've given me some background, I'll often follow up with, "Tell me your faith story," or "Tell me a little about your religious background." These variations are especially helpful if we've already been talking for a while but they haven't shared about their faith, and often I have an opportunity to ask the Platinum Question in the course of our conversation.

"Tell me your story" can be less intimidating for some people than a direct question. It's compelling because

STORY

disapproved and cut ties with her. After that, she walked away from Christianity. Later, she said she realized she didn't walk away from God; she walked away from a poor representation of religion.

She also told me she'd been reading from a well-known spiritual teacher, who draws from many sources such as Buddhism, Hinduism, and Christianity. She said she'd started to ask the universe or spirit for

 CONTINUED . . .

generally people *want* to tell their stories, but they feel they need to be given the permission to tell it.

Listening can do wonders. As an introvert, I'm often nervous that I won't know what to say. But most people don't get asked about their life often and like to share their story, even introverts. People just want to be seen and known.

I use "Tell me your story" because empathy is my top strength. I love the unique design of each person, and hearing their stories allows me to empathize. As witnesses, our goal is often to take people just one step closer to God. By making a caring impression, I give them one positive encounter—to finally meet a Christian who doesn't judge them or hate them but

STORY

things and was starting to see some movement as things began to happen.

Some Christians may have freaked out about her reading extra-biblical material, but I have come to learn God can use anything to turn us toward Him. Instead, I asked, "Andrina, who are you asking?"

She paused and thought and then answered, "I guess it's God."

genuinely cares about them. Most people are not rejecting Christ, but a poor caricature of Christianity.

It's important not to have an agenda in order to establish trust. They need to know you genuinely care and you're not just trying to convert them, or they'll shut down. People can tell whether or not you care about them.

STORY

She'd never talked to anyone about these things before. She'd been on a journey learning about God and life but hadn't had the chance to verbally process what she'd discovered. Questions helped her open up and tell her story.

She is now involved in a foundational Bible study and is connecting with other women from the discussion group.

SOUND BITES

● Find a questioning style that works for you. Practice different approaches and find what makes you most comfortable.

● People can tell if you genuinely care or if you have an agenda.

● People like to tell their stories—listen with curiosity and empathy and they will be open with you.

Compelling questions start by exploring the most significant and testable claims.

Now that we've covered the Platinum Question roadmap, let's examine some other topics and compelling questions that can help you and others in your journey to a better relationship with God. The following chapters will help prepare you for the conversations that will stem from the Platinum Question sequence.

. . . .

If there is a God to be known, where does one begin to research?

. . . .

Why not start with the audacious claims of Jesus, because many religions include Him in some way? Let's start with Jesus and the gospel. Why not start with the most audacious, plausible, and relevant claims first? Jesus and the gospel embody the most significant and testable claims about what we as people ultimately desire and need.

Much of our paralysis in witnessing to others may be due to how little time we spend thinking about the hope of the gospel. If we understand the gospel, we'll feel more prepared to present it to others and to defend it.

When asking compelling questions, will you be ready to explain simply and clearly why you are still a Christ-follower?

Test yourself: Why are you *still* a Jesus-follower? What is your hope and why do you need Jesus?

....

....

....

STORY: A SURPRISE VISIT

The exercise I did with Randy, discovering or creating a God, has been used in other settings.

The question that follows discovering a God is whether God can be known. I told Randy, "The Bible says God loves you and has a purpose, plan, and calling for your life. Next time, I'd like to describe for you as best I can what the New Testament says about this."

Here are my main reasons for hope and why a person should start searching by examining Jesus and His gospel.

Jesus made unique and significant claims. At the end of the documentary *Purple State of Mind*, skeptic John Marks was asked why he continued to explore the claims of Christianity with his former college roommate, Craig. "It's not so much whether it's true; it's the audacity of the claim . . . I want to investigate the *audacity* of the claim."

There are three audacious claims about Jesus:

1. Jesus claimed to be God.

2. Jesus died in our place.

3. Jesus rose from the dead.

STORY

He consented to read a booklet containing four simple points: God's love, man's separation due to sin, Christ's death for our sins, and our response to receive His payment for sins. I left him to ponder our conversation and to make up his own mind.

On Sunday, I planned to deliver a new Bible to Randy. Sunday morning, I was seated for worship at Hope Lutheran Church, waiting to make an announcement

          CONTINUED . . .

Jesus offers amazing grace: salvation as a gift, in contrast to 10 of the 11 major religions, which offer a system of work to merit a place with God.

Jesus' claims are testable and verifiable. We have a wealth of manuscript evidence, containing early eyewitness testimonies; external evidence such as archaeological and non-biblical sources; and consistent internal evidence showing consistency and authenticity of eyewitness claims. Together, these show the strength of the probability of the claims.

Jesus' claims are relevant, livable, and have desirable outcomes. For me and millions, Jesus addresses real needs. Faith in Jesus gives us the following:

• Forgiveness instead of guilt

STORY

for a class I would be teaching, when I heard, "Jon! Jon!" I turned around, and there was Randy!

He asked, "What are you doing here?"

"I'm making an announcement," I said, surprised. "What are you doing here?"

He said, "God told me to come."

- A sense of worth instead of shame and hiding

- Eternal life instead of a perishing life

- God's presence instead of separation and loneliness

- Purposeful, abundant living instead of existential-ism, making up your own meaning

- An account for the existence of evil and suffer-ing, including what causes it (Genesis 3) and how it will end (Revelation 20-22), accompanied by a hope-filled perspective in the present (Romans 8, especially verse 28)

STORY

"Whoa! I'm bringing you a Bible this afternoon. I want to hear all about it."

That afternoon, when I brought him the Bible, I asked, "What happened this week?"

"After we talked Monday, I prayed and asked God to show me a sign if He was really there. Then I took my dog out for a walk in the foothills about dusk. I

 CONTINUED . . .

DO · THIS · NOW

Be ready to explain simply and clearly why you are still a Christ-follower. What are your top 3-5 bullet points about why you have hope?

Share these with anyone close to you to practice.

....

....

....

....

....

....

STORY

crested a hill and there was a lit-up cross a neighbor evidently just put up!"

The cross was perfectly timed, personal, and powerful.

Randy's research began with asking God for a sign and opening his eyes to the possibility of God's existence.

What would happen if more people were prompted to ask God their questions?

People need to know what difference faith has made in your life. Practice sharing your story.

☐ *List your top reasons for why you have hope*

☐ *Share the reasons with someone*

☐ *Tell your story*

SOUND BITES

● Invite people to start their search with Jesus and the gospel, the most significant and test-able truth claims.

● People are more likely to ask about our hope and faith if we are interested in their answers to compelling questions.

● Christ-followers must prepare to give a logical explanation for their hope.

Compelling questions invite everyone to reflect, engage in relationships, and take risks.

• •

What do you fear, ultimately?

• •

There is a lot we can learn from people over 95 years old. In a research study led by Tony Campolo at Eastern University in Pennsylvania, 50 people over the age of 95 were asked what they wish they had done differently in life. Before reading their results, write down how you would answer this question.

....

....

....

....

....

....

There were many answers, but three themes were common:

1. "I would reflect more."

2. "I would take more risks."

3. "I would spend my life on things that would outlast it."

Reflect more. Risk more. Relate more. Put these themes together and you gotta ask, "Am I willing to risk moving toward relating with others to reflect together on these significant God and life questions?"

Why wouldn't we risk it? Unease lurks within many of us, affecting our culture, including Christ-followers. The problem is captured metaphorically in B-52s'

STORY: FIRST STEP

A friend of mine named Charlie wanted to invite an out-of-town friend to a Zoom forum featuring a coronavirus survivor. He was conflicted about the invitation.

The unseen COVID-19 virus was peaking, scaring many as we faced the increasing possibility of death. It was a timely opportunity to explore what happens to us when we die and other faith questions. Even though Zoom makes it easy for a message to access

song lyric, "You are living in your own private Idaho/ Get out of that state/ Get out of that state you're in."

Idaho is alluring to many people. It offers an uncrowded, beautiful place to be. Historically, Idaho virtues feature autonomy, self-reliance, and privacy. Similarly, many people like to live in their own private Idaho, bunkering down with their devices and separating themselves from others without engaging in relationships or sharing ideas.

Our bunkering has the same result as hiding in the trees and foliage in Genesis 3. We still have to face guilt, shame, fear, and blame. We are still perishing— the death rate is 100%. And we're isolated from life-giving relational and spiritual resources.

STORY

many people, wider accessibility doesn't overcome the paralysis afflicting many Christ-witnesses.

Charlie shared the burden of his barrier with our group that was studying relational witness. He said, "I haven't seen or spoken with my friend for six months, but I'd like to invite him to this Zoom forum. It seems abrupt or disingenuous to call out of nowhere to invite him." We explored this problem.

 CONTINUED . . .

Just as God asked Adam in Genesis 3:9, His question is still "Where are you?" The Platinum Question serves to pull the foliage back and expose our nakedness. Bunkered down, relationally separated, and self-reliant, the resources of Jesus Christ do not flow. We need to "get out of that state [of mind] we are in."

As witnesses, we must get out of that state of paralysis in order to help others. Too often we're paralyzed because we feel:

- Guilty about not being a witness

- Unworthy

- Unqualified or unprepared to answer questions

- Uncomfortable with others' beliefs or choices

STORY

"Charlie, why not use the problem of relational separation as your springboard? The man is your friend. You care about him, right?" I asked.

"Well, yes," Charlie replied.

"Why not start there?" I suggested. "You're accusing yourself that you don't care about your friend because you've been separated six months. Disarm the accu-

- Afraid of being rejected

- Afraid of death and preoccupied with this life

At the same time, people who are perishing are feeling:

- Guilt

- Shame

- Fear

- Relational and spiritual separation

- Blaming others

- Being blamed by others

- Spiritual or physical death

STORY

sation by using it as your opening line. Own it first with vulnerability. For example, 'Bill, this is Charlie calling from Boise! I can't believe it's been six months since we've spoken! How are you? What have you been up to?' He'll likely reciprocate. Mention your new experiences: bread-making, coronavirus, and your men's group exploring God and life questions. Mention the

DO · THIS · NOW

Reflect on the similarity between these two lists. What is paralyzing you from becoming a witness of Jesus? Put a check mark next to it. Is there a risk you can take?

....

....

....

....

....

....

....

....

STORY

coming coronavirus Zoom forum. Offer to include him and send the link. Boom!"

Compelling questions invite everyone to reflect, engage in relationships, and take risks. You gotta ask, but you cannot do it in isolation. Don't let your paralysis keep you from asking questions.

. . . END

SOUND BITES

- Compelling questions invite everyone to reflect, engage in relationships, and take risks, including the perishing and the paralyzed.

- Compelling questions, propelled with biblical perspective, help us to break out of witness paralysis.

- Tap into the resources Jesus has given us by engaging with others rather than living in isolation. In isolation, we cannot overcome our fears or paralysis. We need others.

*Compelling questions enable our
witness to be just right.*

. . . .

Why is so much of our communication (including our
witness) in the extremes—too hot or cold,
too hard or too soft?

. . . .

My cowboy friend Dee explained one day, "The key
to understanding and communicating with animals is
knowing they're simply looking for the good place to
be. So you make the right thing easy and the wrong
thing difficult." People are the same.

Recall the story of Goldilocks and the three bears.
She was hungry and entered the bears' empty house
to find three cereal bowls: one too hot, another too
cold, and the third just right. She ate all of the one
that was just right and went on to find a bed that felt
just right.

Like Goldilocks, people are spiritually hungry, needing a place of peace and rest. People with a postmodern mindset are finicky, wanting everything "just right," and as witnesses, we are paralyzed by the possibility we will be too hard or too soft, too hot or too cold in our presentation of the gospel.

Christ-witnesses experience guilt, shame, fear, separation, blaming others, being blamed by others, and death. These seven mountain-sized barriers are paralyzing to the soul.

Notice how Paul answers these seven barriers with perspective in 2 Corinthians 4 and 5:

* *Guilt* – Jesus became our sin and we became the righteousness of God (2 Corinthians 5:21).

STORY: BREAK IT UP

My friend Jeff got into backpack-mountain biking and wants others to experience it as well, not just people who are extremely athletic. He also wants to invite people to explore God and life questions in a shared biking adventure through beautiful Idaho.

For two years, Jeff watched the departure of mountain bikers in the epic Smoke and Fire mountain bike race from Boise to Ketchum and back on mountain

- *Shame* – Our naked, perishing earthly buildings/bodies are replaced by an eternal house (2 Corinthians 5:1-4).

- *Fear* – God has prepared us and guaranteed us His enabling Holy Spirit, and knowing the fear of the Lord, we can persuade others (2 Corinthians 5:5-11).

- *Separation* – The love of Christ controls us, so we are able to lay down our lives for others (2 Corinthians 5:14-15).

- *Blaming* – We see no person as earthly or temporal, but as new creations in Christ (2 Corinthians 5:16-17).

STORY

gravel roads. He tried to imagine what it was like. He questioned if he had the willpower, courage, and grit to participate. Eventually he was compelled to challenge himself, springing him from paralyzed observer to participant.

His first step was to talk to the racers. Then he began to research and train. The first year, he was dependent on mentors and fellow racers for navigation. He

 CONTINUED . . .

- *Blamed* – We are not "canceled" but reconciled with Christ, and God makes His appeal through us as ambassadors (2 Corinthians 5:18-20).

- *Death* – All things physical are temporal; spiritually, we are renewed daily (2 Corinthians 4:16-18).

The points Paul makes have been my "antidote" to paralysis. As we carry the gospel to those who are perishing, we can take heart in these answers to our barriers.

STORY

peddled through miles of grueling terrain and made it to the end.

Beyond the physical hardship, Jeff reflected, "The mental part was the challenge." Now a three-year veteran, his world has expanded, and he is ready to share his discovery. Most of his mountain-biking colleagues do not know Christ.

DO · THIS · NOW

Read 2 Corinthians 5 closely, writing down everything motivating us as ambassadors.

....

....

....

....

....

....

....

....

....

STORY

Jeff will continue to expand his life and passion by spreading the gospel and making friends for the eternal future. His wife, Julie, offered wise counsel, "Jeff, as you think about what you need to do to get to your goal, you need to cut it in half. Then, cut it in half again." With this advice, common people can participate in a challenge that might seem too daunting otherwise.

CONTINUED . . .

*"Christians and non-Christians alike have
something in common. We're both
uncomfortable about evangelism."*

—*Rebecca Pippert*

STORY

Because our mission is creating relational settings to explore compelling God and life questions, Jeff initiated a partnership with me to combine our skillsets. With ten men, we will ride from Boise to McCall and share campfires for two to three days. Amidst relationship building, we'll initiate compelling questions during campfire conversations.

SOUND BITES

- Replace Genesis 3 barriers with 2 Corinthians 5 motivations and perspective.

- People are spiritually hungry and need a place of peace and rest. We can provide that through our witness, using meaningful conversations and authentic relationship.

- God has given us answers to the seven common fear barriers we often face while conversing with others.

STORY

Finding common ground with others allows us to create relational settings where compelling questions can make our witness "just right." By breaking up large ideas into a set of smaller questions, anyone can tackle their significant God and life questions, and we feel confident in our witness knowing that we have a roadmap.

We ask compelling questions because we assume truth can be known.

In our postmodern world, one of the struggles many people face today is whether there is an ultimate truth, and if so, whether it can be known.

. . . .

Is there such a thing as truth, and can it be known?

. . . .

Many people believe that truth is self-defined. We can't agree on what is true, so we accept our own version of the truth. Arriving at shared truth is hard work and seemingly impossible at times.

We're hard-wired for truth. We assume we can know the truth about others, ourselves, and our world. For example, if you accuse someone of being a liar, that carries the *assumption* something can be known truly. Otherwise, what is the basis for discernment or judgment? Therefore, we believe facts can be verified. If someone is not in touch with the truth or actively spins it for their own gain at another's expense, we don't trust them.

Truth by definition is narrow. If you get invited to dinner at 6:30pm, Wednesday, October 15, and you don't receive every detail of the address, including the house number, the street name, and the town or city where the dinner will take place, you will never get there and enjoy the meal and fellowship. If you interchange two numbers and arrive at the wrong address, you may get the door slammed in your face by an annoyed neighbor several blocks away. It doesn't matter that you were close—you had the wrong information, and that led you astray.

It's to our advantage to test claims of truth. The loftier the claim and the more at stake, the more stringent

STORY: OPEN DISCUSSIONS ABOUT GOD AND LIFE

In 2001, 12 Hewlett-Packard employees from multiple Christian faith perspectives explored God and life questions weekly over lunch. For several months in the aftermath of the 9/11 tragedy, people were compelled to seek truth and explore big life questions.

Eventually participants started inviting colleagues to lunch to explore their views. We learned we could have amazing faith exchanges and our gestures of

the test ought to be. But often we need to act even if we're only 75% certain something is true. It's rare to be 100% certain about anything. If you act based upon 75% certainty, it is not a blind-leap, but a calculated step based on the available evidence. So the standard to determine what is true becomes what is *plausible* to believe rather than absolute certainty or 100% proof.

In the next chapter, we'll uncover seven "truth tools" you can use to determine whether something is likely true. But for now, we simply need to acknowledge the existence of truth and that we can know it with some level of certainty. If we didn't believe that truth could be known, we wouldn't bother asking questions. And yet all of us have deep-seated questions about God and life, so we assume that truth about these things can be known.

STORY

friendship were mutual. Conversations were thoughtful, respectful, and forthright. Once we'd established trust with the group, we sought permission to engage a bold initiative.

Motivated to be ambassadors for Christ, we took a big risk and hosted a four-week lunchtime open forum to discuss big questions about God and life. For four consecutive weeks, 35-40 people of every worldview

DO · THIS · NOW

Assess your truth-seeking toolbox. Assuming truth exists, what tools can you utilize to verify the truthfulness or reality of your beliefs?

....

....

....

....

....

....

STORY

participated in an energetic discussion: ages 25-65, women, men, straights, same-sex attracted, Muslims, Mormons, Evangelicals, Catholics, agnostics, atheists, skeptics, protestants, Hindu, Buddhist, everything.

As facilitator, I assumed nothing going into the conversations—after all, it was an open forum. But the flow of ideas week to week was logical. We didn't plan

"Truth will ultimately prevail when there is pains to bring it to light."

—George Washington

STORY

anything, but we intuitively found our way through the following topics:

Week #1 – Is there such a thing as ultimate truth? (We decided there had to be!)

Week #2 – If there is ultimate truth/reality, can anyone know it?

Week #3 – *How* can ultimate truth be known?

CONTINUED . . .

*"In a time of deceit, telling the
truth is a revolutionary act."*

—George Orwell

STORY

Week #4 – Does God have anything to do with it?

Lunch conversations became deeper and more authentic. A focused forum exploring arguments for God's existence followed the conversations. This turned into several break-out groups. It became the impetus for the *Mormon and Evangelical Christian in Conversation* series we later hosted for several years

SOUND BITES

- Competing perceptions of truth can be exhausting, so clarify your assumption about truth.

- We are hard-wired for truth, living as if truth can be known.

- By definition, truth is narrow. Start broad-minded and press for specificity.

- Go for what is probable based on available evidence because 100% proof is rarely possible.

- Faith is not a blind leap, but stepping toward reality based on evidence.

STORY

in homes and at large events. The stories of lives affected still ripples.

Through this story, you can see what happens when compelling questions are asked in relational settings with the assumption that truth can be known.

Compelling questions are best explored with multiple truth-seeking tools.

If truth can be known, how do we go about discovering it? To uncover the truth, there are a number of tools we can use. It's important to understand the tools at our disposal and how they work so we're not led astray.

. . . .

How do we reveal the truth? (First, know you can.)

. . . .

Assuming truth can be known at some level, how do we verify or falsify claims? The seven truth-seeking tools are already in our humanity toolbox. They are gifts of "common grace" from God. Use them all, because all are needed to uncover the truth. Use them well by choosing the right tool for the job.

These are things that we already use in our daily lives—we just have to learn to use them more effectively. Furthermore, we don't have to be experts on every tool, but we certainly want the ability to under-stand each tool's role.

Carrying the analogy further, each of us is like a general contractor on a truth-finding project. We are not experts on everything, but we learn who is and can consult them when needed. Subcontractors, like framers, plumbers, and electricians, have special knowledge and tools. We must understand who we need for each part of the project, and then they must work together.

These tools should liberate us in the quest for truth while being a witness for Christ. We fear being asked questions we cannot answer, but we are liberated knowing a witness is called to share what they know. Expertise is not required. God opens minds and hearts.

STORY: MY PLATINUM QUESTION

The seven truth-tools have been invaluable in my truth-seeking journey. They assisted in answering my question about the apparent obscurity of God: "God, why aren't you more obvious in revealing yourself to us? Why not something more sensational? It's as if you've chosen to be obscure. Why?"

As an ambassador for Christ, if God was more apparent, it would make the job of bearing witness easier.

THE SEVEN TRUTH TOOLS:

Reason (philosophy/logic) – We can determine truth through reason, but we must be careful not to allow poor reasoning to lead us astray.

Legal/Historical (eyewitness testimony/exhibits) – Used in courtrooms and by historians, eyewitness accounts, expert witness accounts, forensics, and exhibits or external evidence are used to build a case for the truth.

Intuition/Personal/Experiential – Intuition is based on our personal surveillance of data, which starts with our subjective knowledge, which we sync up with objective reference points to verify truthfulness.

STORY

Why does this have to be so difficult? It perplexed me for a few years, but I've employed the seven truth tools and encountered enlightening knowledge along the way.

The Tool of Reason - If God were irresistible or irrefutable, it would overwhelm people, making us obligated to follow Him. Because God could easily dominate us, it would violate our free will.

 CONTINUED . . .

Science (empirically verified and repeatable) – Science is great for finding truth about the physical world, but it cannot explore historical events alone because they're not repeatable.

Spiritual/Revelation – We must include the plausibility of God's existence and communication with us as a tool for truth.

Moral/Aesthetic – We have an inherent sense of morality and beauty, things which must be taken into consideration in the pursuit of truth, because science, philosophy, and religion will go rogue without the cross-examination of moral and aesthetic truth-seeking.

STORY

The Tool of Historical Evidence – Practicing sound historiography, the New Testament manuscripts are shown to be authentic and accurate. God gave us enough information to get our attention, but not enough to obligate us to follow Him.

The Tool of Intuition – God lets us experience the consequences of free-will decisions, thus, we experience a world full of evil, suffering, and pain.

- *Community* – Community provides checks and balances by pointing out our biases and assumptions. We weren't meant to seek truth alone.

STORY

The Tool of Science – The testimony of science shouts intelligent design, but everywhere materialist scientists try to skirt it by saying it's not really design. God grants the ability for them to choose their interpretation of the data.

The Tool of the Moral/Aesthetic – On more than one occasion, atheists have said to me their morality is every bit as strong as mine. Why do most humans

CONTINUED . . .

DO · THIS · NOW

Where can you find a group to explore God and life questions? Is there a resource you are compelled to read? Purchase or borrow it.

....

....

....

....

....

....

....

....

STORY

basically share the same moral code? It's God-code. God also proclaims with grand subtlety through the beauty of His creation.

The Tool of Community – Our lives bear witness of the way, the truth, and the life of Jesus to one another.

These truth tools are gifts of "common grace" available to all of us to help us ponder the hiddenness of

SOUND BITES

- The seven truth tools are Reason, Legal/Historical, Intuition/Experience, Science, Revelation/Spiritual, Morality/Aesthetics, and Community.

- We use the seven truth-tools in daily life; understanding these tools will allow us to use them effectively.

- God has great respect for free will—He does not crowd us or force us into believing, but uses these tools to enlighten hearts and minds.

STORY

God. He's given us just enough to test what we really love and long for. We weren't meant to do this alone. Find people who can introduce you to great resources and explore them.

Compelling questions allow voices to be heard.

. . . .

Can we really hear the voice of God?

. . . .

The answer depends on whether we believe Jesus was who He claimed to be: the Son of God. He clearly says so in the face of His enemies in John 10:30, "I and the Father are one."

So can we hear the voice of God? Jesus, who claimed to be God, said yes: "The sheep listen to His voice, and He calls His own sheep by name and leads them out. When He puts all His own sheep outside, He goes ahead of them, and the sheep follow Him because they know His voice." (John 10:3-4)

If Jesus is who He claimed to be, we can have close relationship with God and hear His voice. This book is an invitation and road map to take Jesus up on this bold claim, first for ourselves, and then by guiding others.

The challenge is communicating this message of hope. Can a progressive person believe this? Can a post-modern person believe this? Yes. We are perishing, day by day, and we long for purpose, protection, and the source of our being come to rescue us and take us home. Jesus is the rescuer, and His sheep can hear His voice and follow him.

People who live in the here and now wonder, "How can we believe in someone or something we can't see?" But the reality is we live by faith in the unseen all the time. Consider how often we turn a key, press a button, or flip a switch without seeing or understanding specifically how the mechanics behind it work. Most people don't feel the need to understand how something works before they put trust in it. We

STORY: THE ROUND PEN

A powerful communication happens between a handler and horse in a round pen. "There are many ways to subdue a horse, but that's not the point. The point is communication," my friend Dee explained. We were talking about breaking horses to ride. Then he explained the purpose of a round pen. A square pen has corners, leaving a fearful horse no option but to fight. The round pen allows the nervous horse to

simply know there is good outcome: a light comes on, a car engine starts, or the TV flashes to life.

We can communicate with God—we're coded for it. And we don't have to understand His plan or the way He works to put our faith in Him.

STORY

move freely, while the handler, who wants to build a relationship of trust and respect with the horse, stands in the middle of the pen.

The first signal the handler looks for is the horse watching them with one eye, which signals, "I see you. You appear to be safe." The handler takes a step backward as if to say, "I'm here and I'm not crowding you.

CONTINUED . . .

DO · THIS · NOW

What has been God been saying to you? Who can help you sort out His messages to you?

....

....

....

....

....

....

....

....

....

STORY

I respect you." Then the handler watches for a turned head with two eyes looking at him.

Dee said, "The handler will then turn his back on the horse and walk away from the horse. The horse will follow him. It's as if the horse is holding up a white flag saying, 'I surrender. I trust you. You're the boss.'"

At the library, I found a documentary of a man who practiced the round pen principle with a wild mus-

*"Faith is taking the first step even when
you don't see the whole staircase."*

—*Martin Luther King Jr.*

STORY

tang, but without the round pen itself. For three days, on fresh horses, he stayed in respectful proximity to the mustang and won the right to mount the bridled and saddled mustang. Unbelievable! I had questions for my next coffee with Dee.

"Why would a wild mustang, who can go anywhere and do anything he wants, willingly submit to a man?"

"He wants a leader," Dee answered.

"I spent a long time trying to come to grips with my doubts, when suddenly I realized I had better come to grips with what I believe. I have since moved from the agony of questions that I cannot answer to the reality of answers that I cannot escape, and it's a wonderful relief."

—Tom Skinner

STORY

We are all looking for a leader who is greater than us and who we can trust and respect. I was desperately looking for this leader in the early summer of 1978. My life has been directed by God ever since. I simply needed a leader great enough and good enough to trust.

God used Karen's cemetery question to guide me into the round pen. I circled the round pen for two months. I was not cornered or subdued, just patient-

SOUND BITES

- God created everything. We don't need to know how He works to have faith and communicate with Him.

- Jesus said, "My sheep hear my voice." If He is God, He is able to communicate with us.

- We're all looking for a leader we can trust and respect.

- God doesn't crowd us—He waits for us to come to Him.

STORY

ly invited. He was speaking all along simply by His gracious presence. Now both of my eyes are turned on Him. Like Dee, the horse guide, I want to guide others into relationship with God, starting with a compelling question.

Compelling questions enable us to hear God's voice and guide others to hear it too.

. . . .

How can we hear the voice of God?

. . . .

In the 1980's, Carl Sagan famously opened his series *Cosmos* with these words: "The Cosmos is all that is, or ever was, or ever will be." A naturalist/materialist, Sagan chose these words to capture the immensity and intimacy of the universe.

"The receipt of a single message from space is enough for us to conclude there's an intelligence out there," he said. "Somewhere, something incredible is waiting to be known."

Dr. Walter Bradley, a PhD in materials science and a Christ-follower, added, "And if a single message from space is enough for us to conclude there's an intelligence behind it, then what about the vast amounts of information contained in the DNA of every living plant and animal? Each cell in the human body contains more information than all 30 volumes of the Encyclopedia Britannica . . . the unmistakable sign of an Intelligent Designer."

Why are we skeptical of the unseen when we trust messages from the unseen all the time? Consider how routine it is for us to give and receive specific communication using devices we do not fully understand, with people we cannot see but have reason to believe are there. We do not see who we're communicating with, but we can discern true and helpful voices.

I received a message from someone out-of-state who identified himself as a friend of mine. I know

STORY: HEARING THE VOICE OF GOD

Jim was at the coffee house the first time I invited the table of men to observe me inviting our table-server to answer the Platinum Question. He was the one who asked, "Did you set that up?"

Afterward, Jim began to open conversations with people on the go. One day, he shared a series of conversations he had with our men's group. Jim felt compelled by God to ask people questions. Taking

my friend's voice, even in written text. His comments aligned with my understanding of him and the testimony of other people who know him. I also trust the credibility of the message because of my learned confidence in the technology. I don't see or understand 90% of it, but I use it every day. It's plausible to believe and act on something that is unseen.

Another example is the marvelous human body. How do 70 trillion cells sync up with the human brain, exchanging messages in nanoseconds and enabling your entire body to operate? If God created all of this, He can communicate with us.

So how do we learn to hear God's voice?

Samuel was a young boy serving in the House of God under the tutelage of Eli the priest. One night

STORY

his own spin on the question, he boldly inserted the name of Jesus in the place of God.

While speaking to a bank teller with whom he'd established some rapport, Jim asked her permission to pose an interesting question. When she agreed, Jim asked, "Imagine Jesus Christ was standing right here, right now, and you could ask Him a question and get an answer, what would you ask Him?"

       CONTINUED . . .

God spoke to Samuel, who thought it was Eli calling him while he lay in bed. Twice God called to Samuel. Hearing the voice, twice he ran to Eli thinking he was summoned. Twice Eli sent him back to lie down.

The third time Eli realized Samuel may be hearing the voice of the Lord, so he told him to reply, "Speak, for Your servant is listening." (1 Samuel 3:9-10) When he heard the voice again, he replied, "Speak, for Your servant is listening." And God did. Samuel was able to hear the voice of God because he invited God to speak. (3:11-21)

STORY

In that moment, Jim heard the voice of God. Apparently, the bank attendant heard it as well, because she had an astonishingly emotional response: "Can you forgive me?" They had a brief but amazing exchange about it. It was plainly apparent God was already talking to the young woman, and God had brought Jim into the conversation to help.

I ask the Platinum Question because it's a fire-starter. Jesus said He has lost sheep who hear His voice (John

DO · THIS · NOW

It's our turn to listen. Has He been speaking? "Speak, Lord, Your servant is listening."

☐ *Take time to listen to the Lord today*

STORY

10:16; Luke 15:1-8) and "scattered" sheep He is drawing in (Matthew 18:12-15).

Often, I share the chapter John 10 with both the "gathered" and "scattered," by asking, "Is God saying something to you about a next step He wants you to take? What resistance are you working through to listen and follow?" This question almost always hits the mark: a separated spouse hears the voice to move back in with

SOUND BITES

- We are hard-wired to converse with God, just like our brains send signals to our thumbs as we text messages to friends.

- There are reasons why we do not hear the voice of God. To hear His voice, we must invite Him to speak and then listen.

- God is consistent in His messages, so if in doubt, test what you think you are hearing with His word, the Bible.

- God gives us timely messages and opportunities to bear witness and help others hear His voice.

STORY

renewed perspective; a businessman hears the voice to start a chapel with fellow car-racers at a racetrack; and Jeff wants to share his backpack mountain-biking experience with others and host compelling question discussions around campfires on the trip.

These people heard God's voice to invite others to hear His voice. When people hear God's voice, Jesus gives eternal life to them and they will never perish.

Compelling questions surface pain points that expose our need for the gospel.

The most common responses to the Platinum Question fall into three categories. Almost 90 percent of the time, people want to ask God some version of one of these questions:

1. Why do you allow evil, suffering, and pain to persist?

2. What is the purpose of my life?

3. What do you think of me and how am I doing?

Resources abound to help answer these questions. YouGottaAsk.com is a place to start. You can use these questions to understand someone's pain points and connect them with the gospel.

Compelling questions surface pain points, because we respond to them with whatever is most weighing on us at the time. When you meet someone's pain with empathic listening, you open their heart to new ideas. We know people are open when they ask questions and show interest in resources to help answer their questions. They allow you to become their trusted guide.

It's natural for people to eventually reciprocate our questions and ask us about our lives. This gives us the opportunity to model the gospel to them and tell them about it, starting with how it's relevant to their pain point.

There are many ways we can share the gospel, so a good strategy is to find one you're comfortable with and stick to it. Let it be succinct, clear, and accurate.

In an effort to be succinct and clear, here's a valuable exercise I use to prepare for sharing the gospel.

THE SIX COMPELLING QUESTIONS

QUESTION 1:

Assuming there is a God, and you could ask God anything, what would you ask?

QUESTION 2:

So, of all the questions you could have asked, why ask this one?

Write down the message of the gospel in 25 words or less. Be succinct and clear without abandoning essentials.

....

....

....

Here's my summary:

- God loves every person.

- Our sin separates us from God.

- Jesus's death is a payment for sin.

- Receive Jesus and His pardon for eternal life.

THE QUESTIONS

QUESTION 3:

How would you answer this question for yourself right now?

QUESTION 4:

Do you know anyone who could guide you, or a resource you can consult, to find an answer to your question?

These are four points presented in Paul's letter to the Romans. (Romans 3:23; 5:8; 6:23 and 10:13)

Romans is the most expanded and robust statement of the essence of the gospel. It has grounded my faith and helped me answer the three most asked questions. It's the gospel of God applied to all of life. Therefore, immersing my mind in Paul's letter to the Romans has been transformational and defining for me.

Here's an outline of Romans I memorized as a college student.

- Sin (Romans chapters 1-3)

- Salvation (Romans chapters 3-5)

THE QUESTIONS

QUESTION 5:

Have you ever thought to simply and directly ask God your question?

What have you got to lose?

- Sanctification/Being set apart (Romans chapters 6-8)

- Sovereignty of God (Romans chapters 9-11)

- Service (Romans chapters 12-16)

The book of Romans contains a transformational message of amazing grace. In Romans 8, we find the three themes intertwined answering life's largest questions:

Pain: How we explain evil, suffering, and death is the greatest test of a worldview. "We suffer with Him so that we may also be glorified with Him. For I consider that the sufferings of this present time are not worthy to be compared with the glory that is to be revealed to us." —Romans 8:17b-18

THE QUESTIONS

QUESTION 6:

For you to be a praying person, what would you need God to be like?

What attributes do you need God to possess?

What moral perfections and superpowers would make God "God" for you?

Purpose: When we live without purpose or meaning in the midst of evil, suffering, and death, life is full of despair. We long for meaning in our struggle, and God gives us purpose and meaning. "For in hope we have been saved, but hope that is seen is not hope; for who hopes for what he already sees? But if we hope for what we do not see, through perseverance we wait eagerly for it . . . and we know that God causes all things to work together for good to those who love God, to those who are called according to His purpose . . . for those . . . He also predestined to become conformed to the image of His Son." —Romans 8:24-25, 28-29

Personhood and Performance: We long for value but don't feel valued. The purpose of pain is for the eternal good of the person. "Therefore there is now no condemnation for those who are in Christ Jesus . . . The Spirit Himself testifies with our spirit that we are children of God, and if children, heirs also, heirs of God and fellow heirs with Christ . . . We overwhelmingly conquer through Him who loved us." —Romans 8:1, 16, 37

Romans speaks to a person as a whole: intellect, emotions, and will. It uses all the truth tools to do so: revelation, science-creation, logic-reason, experience, morality, legal-historical, and community.

DO · THIS · NOW

Action 1: Every sentence in Romans 8 addresses the three most asked questions. Underline and color-code each phrase in a slow and thoughtful read-through. Use black for suffering and evil, green for purpose, and blue for identity and value.

Action 2: Listen several times to the BibleProject's Romans overview video. Listen to expositional Bible teachers go through it verse by verse. (BibleProject. com/explore/romans)

Action 3: Memorize these four verses that present the gospel: Romans 3:23, 5:8, 6:23, and 10:13.

Action 4: Read Romans 1-16 for 30 days straight. Yes, you can! It will change your life.

Action 5: Gather a group of cohorts to read, discuss, and master Romans together.

Action 6: Take a reputable online Christian class. Study a couple biblical commentaries to expand your knowledge of the book of Romans.

This immersion in the book of Romans will deepen your understanding of the three most commonly asked questions. You will be better able to explore pain points in conversations and offer guidance.

SOUND BITES

- The most common questions people have for God are about pain, purpose, personhood, and performance. These represent our deep pain points and give us an opportunity to empathize through conversation.

- In the book of Romans, Paul answers our deep life and faith questions and addresses our pain points through a robust presentation of the gospel.

- Find a strategy to succinctly share the gospel in a way you're comfortable with and can easily remember, then practice and use it consistently.

C⬤NCLUSION

*Compelling questions influence a
person's eternal destiny.*

You have a limited budget of time in your life, so let's
get to the point.

We are going to die. It's indisputable.

Each of us choose to live with or without God. When
we die, the soul separates from the body. The soul
either joins God or is separated from God forever.

"For God so loved the world, that He gave His only
Son, so that everyone who believes in Him will not
perish, but have eternal life. For God did not send
the Son into the world to judge the world, but so that
the world might be saved through Him. The one who
believes in Him is not judged; the one who does not
believe has been judged already, because he has not
believed in the name of the only Son of God."

—John 3:16-18

People are perishing.

Do you believe this?

I did, even when I was perishing. But I lived as if I was in control. A sincere and curious question disrupted my illusion of control. It exposed that I was a *slave to the fear of death*, as described in Hebrews 2:15.

What would you like people to say about you at the end of your life?

Here is my list:

- He shared God's amazing grace by showing interest in others, asking curious questions, listening, and circling back to invite others to take a next step toward God.

- He feared and pleased only God (not man), the only one who can rescue people's souls.

- He influenced people to do the same, populating God's kingdom with loved people.

Does part of your list look like mine?

Invite people to use this book to replace paralyzing fear with authentic friendship and compassion. Who can you gather to become a "cohort of campaigners" to prayerfully engage others with compelling questions?

ACKN**⬤**WLEDGMENTS

We'd like to acknowledge those who have walked alongside us through the creation of this book. They are courageous, compassionate, and sacrificial friends. They have helped us figure out how to experience relational evangelism in a swiftly changing culture, and together we are implementing what we believe needs to happen. Without these people, there would be no book.

Our friends who have helped us on this journey are bold. They enable us to live a bold lifestyle and begin the ministry You Gotta Ask, Inc. When we calculated the risk of launching this new organization and mission during 2020, they didn't bat an eye. They said, "Let's go for it." These people are individuals comprising small groups around the community, partners around the country, and life-time friends. We want to recognize them all by name, but we only have a page, so we'll only mention those who have been involved in the making of this book.

First we'd like to thank the Board of Directors for You Gotta Ask, Inc, as well as their spouses, who together supplied bold vision, decision-making, guidance, and refinement of message: Todd and Lisa Kraft, John and Debbie Meyer, Tim and Cindy Winkle, Lee and Kristy Lenhardt, Emmanuel and Tabitha Navarro, Kyle and Lindsay Woods, and Genny and Mike Heikka, co-founder of LIFT for Women, our women's outreach (LiftedHigh.org).

We'd also like to thank the amazing women at Aloha Publishing. Maryanna Young understood the vision of the book and provided guidance in its direction. Maryanna, Heather Goetter, and Megan Terry brought out the best of Jon and Pam, creating a useful and beautiful tool to empower Christ-witnesses. It's been a delightful experience to partner with them in creativity.

AB*O*UT THE AUTHORS

ABOUT PAM

Pam, the Women's Director of You Gotta Ask, Inc., serves in a mentoring role with women throughout the Treasure Valley. She co-founded LIFT, which exists to create impactful, relational events and gatherings that welcome all women and encourage them to live inspired, fearless, and thriving lives.

Pam loves creating safe places for women to openly explore tough questions and life challenges. Her favorite hobby is "soul sloshing"—talking with women over a cup of coffee about matters of the heart. She considers it a privilege to walk alongside women to help them discover and embrace who they are and their unique purpose.

ABOUT JON

Jon is the Executive Director for You Gotta Ask, Inc. Jon has generated "mission startups" including a Christian campus ministry at BYU in Provo, Utah; a church plant (Riverside Community Church) in

Meridian, Idaho; and Search Ministries (national), in Boise. The theme has always been relational evangelism, discipleship, and relational apologetics. Jon loves to train people's hearts and minds, exploring questions about God, life, and manhood. He pioneered the Adventure Dinner, which combines great food shared by interesting people exploring compelling ideas.

Jon refuels in the foothills or along the river, hiking, running, walking, and mountain-biking with routine forays into hot yoga. He loves marking up books to glean ideas, but does his best thinking on the move. He enjoys great stories and learning from the life experiences of other people.

JON AND PAM AND YOU GOTTA ASK

Jon and Pam are the authors of *Spiritual Seeds: How to Cultivate Spiritual Wealth Within Your Future Children* (Elevate Publishing, 2015). This book was dedicated to their four adult sons and daughters-in-law. Though empty nesters, they enjoy three grandsons. Both Jon and Pam were raised in agricultural settings: Pam a Nebraska farm girl and Jon the son of a Montana cattleman and horse-racer. They now grow and train people instead of crops and animals. Together, they co-founded You Gotta Ask, Inc. in the summer of 2020, inviting men and women to take a next step toward God, starting with compelling questions in relational settings.

Made in the USA
Monee, IL
07 May 2021